The Lost Chronicles of Slue Foot Sue

The Lost Chronicles of Slue Foot Sue
And other tales of the legendary

Katherine Hoerth

ANGELINA
RIVER
PRESS

ISBN #: 978-0-9987364-19
Library of Congress Control Number: 2017950147

Cover by Jerry Craven

Angelina River Press
Fort Worth, Texas

For Bruno

Also by Katherine Hoerth

Goddess Wears Cowboy Boots
The Garden Uprooted

Acknowledgments

I am grateful to the editors of the following journals for publishing some of the poems in this book:

Alyss
Autumn Sky Poetry
Bearing the Mask: Southwestern Persona Poems
Beech Street Review
Boundless: Anthology of the Valley International Poetry Festival
Concho Rive Review
Glass Poetry
Langdon Review of the Arts in Texas
Mezzo Cammin: A Journal of Formal Poetry by Women
Orchard
Peacock
Poetry of the American Southwest 2
Poetry South
Southwestern American Review
Texas Poetry Calendar
Voices de la Luna

CONTENTS

Slue Foot Sue

La Sirena

Lobo Girl

La Luna

Slue Foot Sue

The Birth of Slue Foot Sue

A single cornstalk scraped Texas sky.
It burst to life along the High Plain's edge
beneath a covering of black. By morning,
it towered over everything, the trees,
grain elevators, and the Amarillo
skyline in the distance to the south.

A farmhand was the first to see the stalk,
its tassels swaying in the morning breeze
in the middle of the endless cornfield.
He ran to see it, eyes wide with disbelief.
A giant ear was blooming from the stem,
coffin-sized, the bright green hue of spring.
The strands of silk were red instead of gold.

He wrapped his arms around the stalk and climbed,
eager to peel away the husk and glimpse
what grew inside. He gasped in fear and wonder
as he pulled a piece of husk away;
a woman lay asleep, full formed and naked
nestled in a blanketing of leaves,
her auburn hair a tangling of silk.

But as he reached to touch her face, her eyes
shot open and she leapt up to her feet.
Her heart let out a roar that shook his boots.
She stumbled to the earth and galloped off
between the cornrows. *What's your name?* he shouted.

Sue! She yelled, then gritoed with the wind
and disappeared into the rolling plains.

Reports of Strange Happenings Across the West

A tourist out in Palo Duro canyon
claims he saw a giant girl one night
skipping rope along the canyon's lip,
a rope that hissed and rattled as she jumped,
belting out the words to Texico.

A cowboy west of Plainview swears a woman
challenged him one evening to a horserace.
But she was mounted on a giant wildcat
that growled and roared at him, but with her touch
behind its ear, it burst into a purr.
She blew him kisses as he ate her dust.

A girl in Lubbock says she saw a lady
playing hopscotch on the open plains,
creating basins as she skipped. She grabbed
her hand, and side by side the two of them
jumped clear across the moon; the little girl
was found with bits of regolith between her toes.

A child from Odessa swears he played
a soccer match against a gal with legs
as thick and tall as old mesquite trunks.
She wore no shoes. They used a tumbleweed
for a ball, the gaping maw of night their goal.

Earlier this week, reports of mischief
filled the nearby cities, leaving flowers,
glitter, giggles, mayhem in her wake.

This morning, howls rocked the streets of Pecos.
Brace yourselves. She's rolling into town.

Slue Foot Sue Gets a Pair of Cowgirl Boots

No cowboy boots would fit her giant feet:
her ankle bones jut out too far, her calves
too muscular to be contained within the shaft,
her toes too wriggly to fit inside
a box. Instead, she custom-made her own,
skinned the Texas sky to make the leather,
stitched the pieces up with barbed wire fence,
inlayed a couple rays of summer sunshine
gathered from the Rio Grande's surface,
used Guadalupe Peak to make the heel
so she could tower over everyone.
She needed something special for the bootstraps,
something she could use to pull herself
back up when she was pushed into the dust.
She reached into the velvet sky one night
and grabbed a comet, sewed the flaming tail
into her boots and sailed across the moon.

The Geography of Eden

I am the fertile valley to his mountain.
He stands above me, snowcapped, cold and rugged,

lets the mud of everything slide down.
He buries me in silt; I cradle daisies.

I am the planet to his sky. He wraps
clouds around this curvature of earth.

I gaze into him, see infinity,
feel small and insignificant like dust

as I orbit through this great expanse
of black. I am the wilderness, my open

mouth a jungle, dark and deep. His tongue,
civilization, cultivates a garden

with each kiss, macheteing the brush.
His flesh came first; mine filled the gaps. Alone,

my body crumbles underneath the weight
of all the tangled overgrowth, of being.

I am the midnight to his sunny noon.
I am the gala apple of his eye.

Black-eyed Susan

Her name was Black-eyed Susan, like the flower
growing numerous across the prairies.
Lovely and delicate, they grow to be
admired, spread their seeds, then fade away
into the muted backdrop of this landscape.

But Sue was nothing like a flower, fragile,
silent, still. Her lips weren't two soft petals
waiting like wine cups to filled and sipped
from, fragrant, blush and slick. Her hair was never
neat like ringlets of huisache blossoms,
gold and swaying in the gentle breeze.
Her eyes, two flickering stars, were always searching
the horizon for the next adventure.
Her calloused palms, her arms, her sunburnt nape
didn't glimmer underneath the moonlight,
ashen like clusters of Madrone blooms.

Fancying herself more honeybee
than wildflower, Sue would buzz through spring,
imagining her two slue feet, her legs
could carry her away like paper wings
into an ocean filled with Texas sky,
no roots to hold her firmly in the ground.

Starbucks Bravado

While in the Starbucks line, I watch a plague
of grackles on the patio outside
squawking over hunks of old biscotti.
A male ruffles up his feathers, fluffs
his chest to show the world that he's the biggest
as his iridescent body shines,
beautiful beneath the noonday sun.

Inside, I'm worlds away from all that heat
in this land of half-and-half and honey,
fraps and wifi, where the jazz is smooth,
the lights are dim, the scent of coffee fills
the air like jasmine at the peak of spring.

A man belts out the birdsong of his order:

Caramel macchiato, over ice,
a trenta, and quadruple the espresso,

puffs his chest and glances back at me.
He lifts the barbell of his unkept eyebrow,
adjusts his khaki shorts around his belly
that jiggles with bravado as he scoffs.

I decide to order mine to go:

A tall house coffee, hold the cream and sugar.

A scrappy-looking grackle, dressed in brown,
pecks at the cement outside the shop.
Her yellow eyes are on the shimmering feathers
of the male as he struts and flaps.
She feasts on crumbs of sweetness as he preens.

Mr. Trenta sits down at the bar
alone and gulps his coffee through a straw
with beams of sunshine haloing his hair.

Bedhead

Sue's hair is like a patch of wild monte
when she first rises out of bed at dawn.
It's overgrown and fierce, a place to lose
yourself: the sea of swaying wheatgrass, branches
of mesquite, the nests of mockingbirds,
the tangling of old man's beard, the swathes
of weeds, espinas, goat heads, dandelion
fluff, split ends of lava rocks, the curls
of steam unfurling towards the rising sun,
full bushes of acacia filled with thorns
to block escape. Her hair is tall like Chisos
mountains, longer than the Rio Grande
with twice the bends and rapids flowing through,
a mound of rattlesnakes that hiss and strike.

She tames it with a cow tongue cactus pad,
runs her fingers through the snarls and locks.
She pulls it back into a pony tail
to start her day of work and wind and sun.

Sue's Sandia

She has a sweet tooth, wild, insatiable,
an appetite that only mountains fill.
And then she sees it on her kitchen counter—
a watermelon, ripe for slicing open.

The rind is tough like limestone, but she slices
through it with her carving knife, creates
a fault line. Juice erupts onto her hands.
She licks her sticky fingers clean and grins

as she uplifts a hemisphere of fruit
that glistens pink like crystals in the sun
pouring from the open kitchen window.
She slices through again, again, again,

forming pyramids with peaks that tower
above the atmosphere and jagged rocks
that tumble all across her cutting board.
She takes a step back, eying up the landscape—

a waterfall of sweetness, hills of flesh,
caverns filled with seeds. She takes a bite,
gorges herself on planet, sky, and fruit.
She wipes the rivers from her chin and burps.

Eve, the Teenage Years

Once she hit thirteen, their whole world changed.
She refused to trim her hair, a jungle

of locks with vines to swing her fingers from
as she snapped her gum and rolled her eyes

at anything her father said to her.
She started wearing peasant blouses, open,

flowing, and let the breeze goose-bump her breasts.
Her skirts were long and dragged across the floor,

collected dirt and fallen leaves that left
a trail of nature on the sparkling tiles.

She started listening to music, blasted
it in her bedroom to drown out the noise

of his peace. She sang along to songs
she knew would most offend her father's ears.

Her hands were calloused and her feet were blistered.
She didn't want the softness of his privilege,

so she toiled in the garden, worked
until her hands bled even though the table

was full and set especially for her.
She'd grown a taste for everything forbidden—

marijuana, rum, and older men.
She always smelled of earth, patchouli, sweat

and liked the way it clashed with the cologne
he spritzed on every morning as he dressed

in his suit, his tie, his polished shoes.
At night, she'd dream of leaving their neat home;

she felt it mock the chaos in her heart.
The window beckoned her, the breeze called out

her name, a serenade to leave it all,
to slough her clothes and jump the picket fence

of Eden, disappear into the night,
and let the urban jungle swallow her.

It Happened Along the Rio Grande

Love was an abstraction, like the single
heart-shaped cloud adrift within the ocean
of the open Texas sky in summer.

She thought of this while racing up the current
of the Rio Grande, straddling
her giant catfish as it leapt above
the rolling waves, the dorsal fin in one
hand and her trusty pistol in the other.

She'd always been alone among the crowds.
She liked her freedom, answering to no one
but the wild voices in her heart.

The river curved, a tangle of mesquites
were just ahead, a place of shaded respite
from the heavy-handed sun. And there,
standing on the bank, a silhouette
of a man, a cowboy hat, broad shoulders,
his horse was lapping up the beryl water.

Something in her made her stare. She liked
the way the sun had turned his skin to leather
like her boots, tough and made to last
through her adventures. His face was glistening
with sweat like morning dew. His jeans fit tight.
She bit her lip and smiled a guileless smile.

Her catfish bucked. *Yeehaw,* she yelled as loud
as she could muster. Mountains shook, the waves
kicked up. The cowboy caught her gaze and grinned,

and as she saw the sweat-stains on his shirt,
she lifted up her pistol towards the sky
and shot a hole inside that heart-shaped cloud
to let it pour sweet rain and wash him clean.

Romance at High Noon

The next day she returned to that same place,
the river's curve, at high noon when the sun
made anything but rest impossible.

She sat beneath an old mesquite tree.
Its branches, slouching in the rushing water,
gave just a touch of shade to cool the earth,
her skin, but not her heart. She kicked her boots
off, stuck her calloused feet into the river,
and hummed a song that came straight from the birds,
the bees, a song that she imaged primrose sings
in June. He would come; he had to come
to this same place to find her once again.

She thought she'd seen a sparkle in his eye,
she thought she saw a smile, a flirty wink,
or maybe it was all inside her head.
All her life she'd heard that men prefer
their girls like wildflowers, delicate
and waiting to be plucked. But she was more
like thunder in the sky, a hungry panther
in the canyon, or a mustang running
through the prairie beautiful and free.

She'd hollered loud enough to shake the Chisos.
She knew he'd heard her, seen her perfect shot,
and felt the rain run down his sweaty back.

He wouldn't come to her, she was convinced.
She closed her eyes and leaned against the trunk,
resigned herself to living life, a tumbleweed
that roams the endless countryside alone.
She couldn't change, and anyway, why bother?

And then she heard his footsteps in the dust.

Love Poem to Big Tex

I used to love you like a woman loves
a god, my Helios in cowboy boots.
I'd gaze into your eyes like distant stars
and marvel at their brightness and perfection.

Who wouldn't fall in love with you, a pillar
of everything it means to be a man:
the vast expanse of pecs and rolling biceps,
your rugged Dickies with their twenty-seven-
foot waist, a face as tough and still as stone.
Your shoulders carried an infinity
of Texas sky. Your booming voice, your drawl,
brought me to my knees to kiss away
the prairie dust in worship from your boots.
There I'd feel so small and lose myself
within your looming labyrinth of shadow.

They say it's dangerous to love a man
this much, to fall into his arms this hard,
but what about the image of a god?

The sparks began one morning in your boot,
consumed your denim, shirt and hat in minutes,
blazed like rage across your perfect body,
reducing it to rubble, ash and smoke.
Your face became a molten river, fluid
with fear and traces of humanity.
Even from a distance I could feel
the flames, their warmth like breathe against my cheek.
I watched in awe and wonder as you fell.

Now, they say you're bigger than before—
a new colossus, risen from debris,
but I know you're mortal just like me.
You topple in the midst of heat and pressure.
You tumble to the ground when faced with years
of carrying the weight of everything.

Big Tex, it only makes me love you more.
You're sexier when crumbling, smoked and singed.

Watching the Sunset, Slightly Buzzed

You're gonna be the man I marry, Bill,
she said before he'd muttered his last name.
It didn't matter, nothing did except
his raspy voice, the tilting of his face
the scent of earth he carried on his skin
that made her sure of everything and nothing
all at once. She took another swig
of whiskey from his flask and watched the sunset,
noticed how it framed his silhouette
in gold and made him look just like a god
in a cowboy hat. He told her legends,
how he'd tamed the West, a trusty pistol
and a rope in hand. But as the daylight
faded from his face, he looked more man
than legend with wide eyes that interlocked
with hers. He saw them as two spinning cyclones
come to sweep him off his feet and carry
him into the chaos of their love.

She leaned in, kissed him, tasted earth and whiskey.
She knew that he would be the death of her.

Sue Beneath the Stars

They lie together underneath the moon,
the indigo of night, a thousand stars.
She feels the campfire's breath, his sweating hand
in hers, but still the desert breeze is cold
against her naked skin. His face is full
of starlight as he tells her she deserves
the world and more, a man whose heart is bigger
than a legend written in the rugged landscape,
a million stars to shine around her finger.

Gunshots drown the songs of katydids,
and one by one the stars all tumble down
onto the dusty earth and in his arms.
The sky is almost soot. The North Star burns
alone, illuminates the cloudless sky,
the empty prairie, and his eyes that gaze
at her, see nothing else. He tongues his lips.
She grabs her gun and points it towards the sky.
The velvet blanket of the night falls down,
covering them in a quilt of darkness.

Kitty Leroy Proposes Marriage

Let me shoot an apple off your head;
it's the only way to prove you're right
for me, the only way that we can wed.

You know my reputation, what's been said
about the way I handle guns, my tight
grip. I can shoot an apple off your head

with both eyes closed, half-drunk, in heels instead
of boots. So let me have a go tonight.
If you survive, my darling, we'll be wed.

The chamber's belly's loaded up with lead.
Now all you have to say is yes, to bite
the bullet with my gun aimed at your head

to prove your love and trust in me. I said
that I don't need a man who's rich or bright.
I need a man with balls of steel to wed

a crazy gal like me. I aim, I spread
my legs, I close my eyes and dream of night.
Just let me shoot that apple off your head.
If we survive, my darling, we'll be wed.

Summer Nights

Summer meant the nights were too short to leave her
satisfied. She wanted to swallow moonlight
as it poured down onto the peaks of mountains,
wanted to swallow

darkness as it fizzled along the edges
of horizons, tasting the wind on sunburnt
skin at dusk. She wanted to feel the cacti—
cholla and prickly

pear, against her lips and to taste agave,
gaze in yellow eyes of their open flowers—
moan like toads at midnight emerging after
slumbering all day,

shriek like owls riding the gusts of desert
wind, and howl like the coyotes in her
wild heart. She wanted to feel the landscape
under her body,

feel the weight of clouds on her hips, and wrap her
arms around the world as it spun. But summer
nights are short. The sky has to zip its darkness
up before dawn breaks,

leaving her alone and unquenched. She takes a
sip of morning dew from the winecups blooming
all around her, blushing magenta in the
prairies of wheatgrass.

Pecos Bill, the Morning After

The legends told about old Pecos Bill
were exaggerated. Tales were taller
than the man asleep beside her, more
chihuahua than coyote. On the floor,
their boots laid side by side, but his were dwarfed
by hers. And though the stories go he rode
his horse, a cyclone, and wildcat all day,
his stamina was not enough to satisfy
the appetite of Slue Foot Sue. She woke,
and gazed across the vista of his body,
his arms like rattlesnakes, his chest a valley
filled with curly brambles that kept his heart
hidden underneath a swathe of black.

But unlike all the lovers of her past,
he didn't run away when faced with mountains
to climb, her body's wide expanse of prairie,
pocked with cacti needles, hidden basins,
her mouth a howling cavern filled with wind.
The thunder of her snoring afterwards
didn't even make him flinch. She breathed
a sigh of morning breath and felt a smile
unfold across her blistered lips. She leaned
in for another taste of dust and kissed
him so he'd wake. His eyes were butterflies,
open, soft and umber. He touched her cheek,
a flush of morning sunshine bathed her flesh.

But when he dressed and dawned his cowboy hat
he walked out of her bedroom with a saunter
of a legend, head held high, a cocky
grin that made her want to strip it all
away and see him naked once again.

Slue Foot Sue to Pecos Bill

All the things you've done to prove your love!
You've snuffed out all the fires in the sky
and in your heart to let one burn the brightest
in the indigo of night. You've lassoed
spring to make a sweet bouquet for me
of bluebonnets, marigolds and prickly pear.
You've got down on one knee with just a promise,
offered me the diamond of your eye.

But none of this, dear Bill, is good enough.
To love me is to let me be your equal,
ride at your side, not clinging to your waist.
Step off that high horse, let me in your saddle.
Show me that you're man enough to love
a woman with a will as strong as yours.

West Texas Love Sonnet in Blank Verse

Pecos Bill agreed to marry Sue
if she would only do the following:
always ride double at his back, slough off
her jeans like snakeskin and emerge a flower
on the prairie blooming just for him
with hands like petals, soft, the callouses
sliced off, the dirt beneath her fingernails
scrubbed clean so he could feel her tender touch,

to let him be her knight in shining buckskin
come to save her from herself, to slay
the mountain lions growling in her throat,
so he could show the cowboys how he tamed
the wildest of the west, the monte nestled
inside the raging heart of Slue Foot Sue.

Love in All Seasons
For Sara and Rodney

I.
Everybody falls in love in spring.
It's easy with the pollen in the air,
sun peeking through the slate clouds, shy or coy
at first, a smile held back, about to burst
into radiance. The naïve come,
eager to work their clean hands through the soil.
Your garden gloves are stiff. A price tag dangles
from your sunhat. You tuck the tiny seeds
into the earth and water, wait, then dump
Miracle Grow, although the earth's already
wet with dew and love. The first bud opens
its petals, slips into the lips of March.
The world is different now. The flowers bloom
in every corner of your lovesick mind.

II.

In summer, there is more of everything.
You feast on what the season has to offer—
the sun's embarrassment of riches streaming
down to feed the flowers, large as grinning
faces, already drunk on their own nectar,
tropical rainstorms tumbling ashore
to wet the fertile, sodden soil, the days
that almost seem to never end. You spend
them in your garden, clipping, digging, planting.

Your garden drinks you in, the sweat that rivers
down your back, the soft touch of your hands
the dirt beneath your fingernails. For love,
you toil with a smile as bright as June
dreaming of those cool and humid nights.

III.

Her love in autumn's just as beautiful.
It enters with a sigh of satisfaction
at the heavy, heaving branches filled with fruit
that you produced together hand in hand.

You stop to pluck one, hold the blazing fire
of an orange in your calloused palm,
a star that's made of life, of sweat, of love,
of everything the two of you can offer.

You peel it, let the flesh dissolve into
your tongue, and taste the sweetness of tomorrow.
You'll savor this together underneath
October's sky that rumbles, warns the world

of what's to come. Breathe deep, take in the smell
of fallen leaves returning to the earth.

IV.

The few who love in winter know a love
that's deeper. Every petal's fallen; fruit
has been devoured, savored. Branches hang,
naked, brittle, but you come to listen
to the beauty of them rustling in the wind.
You wander through the garden, tend the hollies
with gentle streams of water. Now, you run
your fingers through the soil because you've grown
accustomed to the smell of earth on skin.
She's nothing left to offer but herself.

May your marriage always be of this—
cherishing each other through the seasons,
flourishing together hand in hand,
loving simply for the sake of love.

Eve at the Art Museum

I used to feel a certain freedom, naked,
wandering my garden, letting sunshine

pour on my shoulders, windstorms brush my hair,
dew drops wash my toes with every step.

My soles were tempered by the pebbles, palms
from pulling up the endless cow tongue seedlings.

I thought my flesh was everything we needed,
nothing more and nothing less, my thighs

the foundation, thick like weathered trunks
of oaks, my stomach soft, a place for him

to lay his head, my nipples firecracker
blooms, a place of nourishment. My shadow

loomed, a silhouette of coolness, swathe
of respite from the sun. I thought my body

was a part of paradise that moved
mountains of rocks, weeded clean the jungles,

making flowers burst into their glory.
Who would have guessed a painter would be watching

me between the chain links of my Eden?
He dipped a brush into his painter's palette

recreated me to match the image
in his mind, his dreams, a thing of beauty

made for gazing at with alabaster
skin, no trace of sunburn, hair a rolling

river of curls with every single strand
in place, my belly nothing but an empty

bowl, no fruit remaining to be tasted?
Who knew that everyone would stare and marvel

at this body, celebrate its beauty, not
its strength, the way it heaves and muscles, sweats

nourishes, creates new worlds from flesh.

Sue, Dressed to the Nines

Her wedding dress was custom made for her.
It had to be, for Sue Foot Sue was not
a cookie-cutter kind of gal. Her body
was the wild west, her curves the winding
of the Rio Grande, the peaks of Chisos
at her chest, her back small slopes, a valley.
Her dress was yellow like the fields of prairie
sunflowers, blooming everywhere in summer,
at her ankles, all across the hills
and in her heart, an opening of petals.
Her hair was like a wildfire, burning
flash of red out of control beneath
a tiara made of rhinestones, sparkling
in the heavy Texas sun. Her dress was fitted,

the bodice dug into her skin, and strapless
to show off her beautiful broad shoulders
and the guns she never had to load,
bronzed from working on the range all day.
Just beneath the hoopskirt of her dress,
she hid her rugged pair of cowboy boots,
the only pair of shoes she'd ever worn
and felt herself, a pistol strapped beneath
a garter made of lace, for just in case
all Hell broke loose. And then, of course, she wore
a bustle, round and heavy at her back
that bounced with every giddy step she took.

Wedding March

The only thing he told her not to do
was ride his Widow-Maker—*He's too wild
for a girl, you'll hurt yourself, my love.*

But Sue had never thought herself a girl.
She was a woman, beautiful and strong.
If he saw her riding down the aisle,
perhaps he'd learn to love her as an equal.

So with her corset tightened and her bustle
fastened, as she heard the wedding march
begin to chime, she tiptoed to the stables,
found Widow-Maker saddled up to go.
She smiled a guileless smile, knew what to do.

As the wedding guests were whispering
and wondering where Slue Foot Sue could be,
she busted down the aisle atop the horse,
his galloping, her hollering and hooting,
drowned out the ringing songs of wedding bells.

The guests were shrieking, laughing at the sight.
At the altar, Pecos Bill called out
Get off that horse, you woman! Get off now!

Then Widow-Maker freaked, began to buck,
jump, and snarl. But Slue Foot Sue held on
and laughed, held on with just one hand
to show the cowboys and her love that she
was made of tougher stuff than taffeta
and silk. She hollered twice as loud and gazed
into her lover's eyes that burned with fear
for her; his cheeks were flushing like the sunset.

And that's when she decided to let go.

Sue, Over the Moon in Love

Slue Foot Sue comes crashing down to earth,
a feisty ball of fire and flesh, her arms
outstretched like angel wings. She hits the ground
butt first, her bones meet jagged rocks, her eyes
meet nettles as a cloud of dust kicks up.

The bustle bounces, sends her towards the sky.
A rush of wind rips her tiara off;
her hair becomes a wild mess of tangles.
Petals tumble from her outstretched hands.
She sails through clouds and tastes them with her tongue;
she glimpses heaven just above their surface.
Gravity tugs her as she somersaults
to earth, re-entering the atmosphere
a meteor with a trail of lace and fire,
landing near Odessa, bustle-first,
and rippling the earth. But there stands Bill,
his trusty rope of rattlesnakes in hand
orbiting overhead. Before the ground
can swallow her inside its throat of rocks,
she bounces up again to taste the sky,
looks down at Pecos Bill who throws the rope
towards her in hopes of bringing back his love
into his arms. But Sue is wilderness,
won't let the lasso wrap around her waist.

She reaches towards the beckoning sky, her body
like a rocket, burning bright and aiming
for the stars. She busts through clouds and glimpses
her face within the craters of the moon,
frontier as wild and dark as her own heart.

Bill, Awaiting Sue's Return

This wasn't how the story was supposed
to end: an empty lasso, empty arms.

The object of his love had disappeared
with spring. A summer so damn dry that nothing

bloomed but blisters on his sunburnt skin
replaced her. Night, the only respite, brought

a howling wind that sounded like her voice,
the moonlight sheening like her eyes, the shadows

of coyotes slinking through the night
he swore were hers. Was that her quiet knocking

at the door? Was that her humming or
a nightingale? Each rustling tumbleweed

was her lost footsteps floundering through the darkness,
making her way home and to his arms.

She was daybreak, opening the door,
her bright red locks of hair igniting morning,

lighting up the prairies and his face.
He waited for her like a yucca waits

for the heavy scent of petrichor
that never comes. He swallowed sadness down

his throat like jagged bits of cinnabar,
like a man. He practiced his goodbye

on the lissome silhouettes of swooping
peregrines, broke up with horny toads

that skittered cross his path, that lonely road
out of Pecos leading him to nowhere.

Her heart beat was the sound of boots on dust.

La Sirena

The Choice

Contemporary mermaids have a choice:
you live on land and find your one true love
or stay beneath the waves and to keep your voice.

First of all, be grateful and rejoice
that you have options. All the mermaids of
another generation had no choice;

waves pushed her to the shore, her tail destroyed
by jagged rocks. Stranded on the cove,
she had no choice but to give up her voice,

and hope to find a sailor who enjoys
a woman's beauty and her charm above
all else. But now, my dear, you have a choice;

the ocean is your oyster. Just avoid
the surface, tell the sailors all to shove
off, keep your independence and your voice,

and drown yourself in loneliness. The price
is steep. Your tail and your voice for love,
the open sea for land's embrace, the choice

is yours to make. You want to keep your voice
and have it all? You want a man to love
you, loud and free? That's cute. Now make your choice.
Do you want love or do you want your voice?

Eve at the Home Depot Garden Center

She breathed in deep the smell of fertilizers,
bug sprays, the staleness of recycled air,
while wandering through the aisles of the store
where everything was carefully manicured
to bloom, to thrive, to catch the eyes of men.

She'd planned to buy a couple apple trees,
but their leaves were yellowed from the sun,
and even with the sale they cost too much.

All around her, conversations buzzed:
Which pesticide is best to kill the aphids?
How to keep the mockingbirds away?
How much to prune to yield the fullest roses?

How can this be paradise? she wondered,
fingering the daisy petals, dyed
in every color of the Skittles rainbow.

She shielded her eyes and squinted past the aisles
beyond the parking lot, the busy highway
to the monte where the lovegrass swayed,
grew three feet tall, a rolling champagne ocean.
Grackles glided overhead, their plumage
iridescent in the Texas sun.
The licorice scent of anise rode the wind
and beckoned her. In the middle of the meadow,
a persimmon tree stood six feet tall,
its branches heavy with the weight of ripened
fruit about to tumble to the earth.

She licked her lips, abandoning her cart,
the garden, paradise, for something sweeter.

Buffalograss in the Schoolyard

This is what their world is like before
they get mowed down—a gentle gust of wind,
they sway in unison to silent music,

rippling like water. They hold hands
underneath the loam and speak a tongue
of giggles no one else can understand.

They keep secrets hidden in their blades;
a fledgling wren keeps still and holds her breath
as a coyote splits the sea of grass,

hungry but oblivious to what
they veil within their soft embrace of green.
The future looms—an open sky, so vast

they grow like weeds to fill the space and split
their flags like fingers into peace signs, spread
their tiny seeds like rumors to the breeze.

They thrive together here in paradise
until they grow too tall, as high as hips.
The gardener will trim them down to size.

First Catcall

You were the goddess of your neighborhood,
the streets where you grew up—the queen of asphalt,
destroyer of all silence with your giggling,
savior of drowning bugs in puddles, bringer
of spring, the season riding on your shoulders
sunflowers popping open with your smile.

One summer afternoon, you walked the dog,
your head in paradise, held high and gazing
past the curvature of earth. A truck
slowed down, disturbed your peace. *Hey sexy thing*

the driver shouted out his rolled-down window.
You made the grave mistake of looking him
square in the eye as though you were a mortal
human being. *How old are you?* he asked.

You were twelve, but didn't say a word,
instead, just breathed the heavy scent of fumes,
felt it fill your throat with breathlessness.

You tugged your dog and ran away towards home.
Well fuck you then. The truck sped off and roared.
You tasted fear and swallowed it like stones,
its sour tang a flavor you would learn
to savor, an acquired taste, because
this paradise was never yours to claim.

Cashier Girl

A man comes up to me to buy his porn.
It's my first day working at the bookstore.
My hands are shaking at register.

I pick my glitter nail polish; tongue
strawberry flavor from my shiny lipgloss.

I'm trying not to touch the porn. I'm trying
not to look down at the woman on
the cover of that dirty magazine,
that pair of eyes that gaze straight into mine.

I try not to look up at the man
who stares at me. I scan his magazine.
It doesn't register.I have to search
for the barcode. This takes time. The man
jingles coins inside his pocket, taps
his foot, and asks me questions just to fill
the silence—

    How long have you worked here, darling?
Where you from? And do you have a boyfriend?

I ring the magazine up as he asks -
How old are you?

    I'm seventeen.
                      I mutter
as I look down at my scuffed-up shoes.
I clear my throat. I hear my thumping heart.
The register lets out a ring and opens -
demands ten dollars.

    Oh, that's cool, he says
Probably just a little younger than
the girls inside my dirty magazine.

All I can do is giggle as I blush.
I slam the register, hand him his porno,

forget to take his money. He walks off,
his head held high, smug smile on his face.

I'm left ten dollars short when my shift ends.
I bit my lips until they turn from pink
to plum.
         My new boss scolds me, asks what happened,
but I pretend I'm just a bimbo who
can't count, do basic math. He threatens me,
says he'll fire me if I slip up.

It was the first day of a job I'll keep
through all four years of college, one that pays
for my tuition, a job I grow to love.

The Mercedes Outlet Mall, After Christmas

Because the season left me feeling empty,
because the billboards flashed across the night,
because the promises were miracles

of sales and clearance prices, I made the journey
to the outlet mall, the glittering mecca
for the label-conscious and the broke

alike. I'm ushered in by sparkling lights,
the smell of fresh baked cookies, and the signs
advertising savings. Here, I come

to hear the songs—the rustling of plastic
bags, the whines of children wanting more,
unzipping purses, rings of open tills.

There's images of models plastered on
the walls of every store, awash in light,
ethereal and warm, displaying fashions

that I emulate with imperfection
as I try on boots and skinny jeans,
decide to buy a pair 'cause, what the hell,

there's something sacred in the way my ass
looks in the mirror of the dressing room,
and I convince myself I'm worthy of

a gift. Still, I feel a quiet rumbling,
a need for more, a Great American
Cookie, the warmth of Starbucks coffee slipping

past my lips, and so I buy, consume,
my belly full, my mouth sweet. Just before
I go, I toss my last two pennies in

the fountain, make a wish, a final plea,
and listen to their splash. I leave the mall
feeling just as empty as I came.

Pizza Buffet Day Dream

Life's a great buffet; you eat your fill
and leave. I think of this while waiting in
the line and eying up the row of slices—

pepperoni, veggie, double cheese.
My stomach moans in hunger and desire
as I imagine filling up my plate

with stacks of slices, two from every pie,
making pizza sandwiches, supreme
between two deep-dish mushrooms, slathering

everything with generous gobs of ranch.
I'll go back for seconds, thirds, and fourths;
I'll lick my lips and fingers when I'm done.

I'll leave this place with pants a little tighter
around the waist, with pores that overflow
with grease, a face that shimmers in the sun,

a scarlet stain of marinara sauce
to let the world know I enjoyed myself,
and savored every naughty, saucy bite.

The Goddess on Laundry Day

The day has come; she's let it get so bad
she's down to her last pair of underwear.
She heaves a sigh while staring at her pile,
a mountain made from all of her mistakes.

She knows this task is going to take all day—
washing the scent of last night from her bedsheets,
the scarlet stain of marinara sauce
that seeped into her stretchy yoga pants,
the smell of smoke that soaked into her bra,
the coffee from her bathrobe that she wore
for three days straight, the beer she spilled all over
her skinny jeans, the stench of his cologne
fouling her favorite dress, the one
she wears too often when she wants to feel
beautiful when looking in the mirror.

But after laundry day, she'll have a chance
to get this right again, to sort the chaos
of her wardrobe out. She separates
the colors from the whites, the delicates
from her unmentionables. She pours the bleach,
the soap. She lets the washer flood with foam.
The drain will swallow all the dirt away.

The dryer belts a song of victory.
She pulls her satin bedsheets out; they catch
the laundromat's florescent light and shine.
She holds them to her nose and takes a whiff
of bleach, of lavender, of nothing else.

She promises tomorrow will be better,
to never let her laundry basket fill.
She promises, she promises, she swears.

Eve Cleans Out Her Fridge

Today's the day she'll throw it all away.
So much she keeps that only takes up space
inside her cluttered fridge and tangled psyche!

Her hips are sick of being compared to pears.
She throws them all away. Her breasts are tired
of being melons, honeydew or musk.

She throws them all away. Her skin was never
cream, and anyway, she'd let it curdle
weeks ago. She dumps it down the drain.

She hated being just a piece of meat—
her thighs a juicy chicken thigh, filet
migon her flesh. It's moldy and expired.

She throws it all away. The Splenda-sweetened
yogurt made her gag. The diet soda
tasted like crap. The rice cakes all were stale.

She throws it all away, the food that left
her stomach yearning, labels promising
to shrink her down to the ideal size.

She scrubs the shelves until they sparkle, bare
and beautiful. She shuts the door and heaves
a heavy sigh of tired satisfaction.

There's almost nothing left to weigh her down
except an apple sitting on the counter.
It's something she could never throw away...

Sleeping Beauty Cantaloupes

Observe these globes of sweetness nestling
together as they ripen underneath
the abundant Pecos sun. Imagine
spending a lifetime hanging on the vine,
cheek to cheek and rind to rind. They bask,
rotund and filled with beauty, seeds and juice.
Do you imagine cantaloupes are dreaming
of the moment they'll be plucked, the kiss of knife,
the slicing of meridians, the sucking
dry of juice, the roll of tongue on honeyed
fruit, the gnashing teeth, the languid slide
down the hatch, the moan? But don't be fooled.

This sleeping beauty dreams greater things
than being pleasing to your greedy tongue.
As she slumbers in her naked glory,
she thinks of dulcet rain, the moistened earth
around her roots, the beaks of kisskadees
carrying pieces of her ginger flesh
into the blushing sky, becoming sun,
her seeds dispersing through the rugged brushland,
another generation made of sweetness
and plenty, of thriving in this ruthless landscape.

Hurricane Woman
For Janis Joplin

She lived her life out like a hurricane
forming in this bustling oil town
where a thin veneer of loveliness,
of picket fences, perfect lawns and churches,
covered up the smog and poverty.

She felt the endless Texas sunshine mock
the clouds within her heart. Her voice was thunder,
drowning out the chirping choir on Sundays,
belting out a melody of truth.

They said she was too loud, she took up space.
She couldn't change, she sunk into depression
in the ocean of her isolation.

She let her hair grow wild, a tangled beauty
spilling like oil across her sunburnt shoulders.

They called her sinner, ugly bitch and whore.
She sucked it up like gulfstream waters, warm,
the perfect fuel to feed the growing storm
of her blues. She kicked up waves with every
song she sang out on the seawall, feet
dangling above the ocean spray.

She was too brash, too fierce, too powerful
for the levees of that sleepy town
to keep under control or understand.

Eventually, she rolled onto the shore,
made landfall, ripping through Port Arthur's peace,
churning liberation and destruction
with her voice, her whipping winds of change.

Then, she head out west and went the way
of hurricanes. She drifted, poured her soul
into thirsty hearts across the land.

She made them sway; she made them open up
their mouths and sing along, each song a raindrop
rolling down the forehead of the world.

A Construction Site in Spring

This story's almost a cliché. The air
thickens with sun, the distant scent of rain,

the desperation in the mating songs
of mockingbirds. Construction workers lunch,

perched atop a liquor store and fill
the world with scents of tar and sweat, the boom

of laughter and their presence. You, a woman,
cross into their gaze, a slit of sunray

streams between two clouds of indigo.
You're suddenly aware of your reflection

in the fingerprinted window—skin
is rusk and smooth, your hair is rustling,

wild, wavy, snarled and iridescent.
Your gypsy skirt is dancing at your ankles.

Your body braces for the imminent
call of spring, that bittersweet reminder

of your place within this world, the natural
order—construction workers, made to catcall

from above like bumble bees were made
to visit buds of lavender, like mice

were made to snugly fit inside the maw
of a cat, like lovely mortals made

to fill the lust of gods from thrones of clouds.
You hurry past, eyes on your feet, the cracks

in the cement, the red ants marching off,
carrying bits of green. You're met with silence,

not even a whistle. Your heart sinks
as you look up at the men, their legs

dangle from the roof's lip as they chat,
their eyes fixated on the pile of shingles,

dizzying swathes of sky, the brilliance
of life that pirouettes around you all.

One notices you staring, waves as though
you're just another human being. You chuckle,

shake your head, walk on your merry way,
wondering if perhaps you're getting old.

Helen Finds a White Hair

Another spring greets Helen as she blooms
as beautiful as ever at her window.

She unties her braid. The sun breaks through,
illuminates her iridescent strands

that sheen like feathers of a hummingbird.
Today, the breeze is thick with citrus blossoms;

the endless sky above is blue and vast.
Helen sighs. She's seen it all, what spring

becomes, this time of beauty, wriggling free
from winter's icy fingers, summer's heat

nipping at its heels as it runs.
She knows as soon as spring begins, it ends.

Helen runs her fingers through her hair;
a couple strands come loose. They catch the sunlight,

bold and golden like a daffodil
whose scent attracts the bees that come with stingers,

pollen drunk and desperate for a taste,
whose hue calls out to hummingbirds that fence

each other for the nectar that it holds
tight inside its whorl, whose beauty brings

the boys who come to pluck them from the ground—
all this chaos stemming from a flower.

She throws them one by one into the wind.
Leave such beauty to the birds, she ponders

to herself and shakes her lovely head.
A single strand is white instead of gold.

Her stomach drops. She thinks of all years
of golden hair behind her, all the years

of gray ahead. A sudden smile blooms.
She wonders if the daffodils rejoice

as their petals fade from gold to brown,
as each one falls to earth when spring is over,

how they ease into the quietness
and fall into the slumber December,

the meadow filling up with peaceful snow
and turning alabaster like her hair.

The Legend of Sirena

I.

I've washed up on this shore of hopelessness.
I'm staring out into the waves that promise
to cover me in foam and pull me under,
clothe my flesh in kelp, and keep me hidden
from their gaze that fills me now with shame.
You should have seen my skin before the algae,
tanned and tough, the color of the earth.
You should have seen my legs before this change,
strong like cypress trunks; they carried me
faithfully with grace across the plains.

I didn't know that I was made to be
an object of desire. I had a hunger
all my own. I loved a handsome man
with midnight hair, a face as soft as loam.
His name was Ollokot. I loved him but
a woman doesn't choose who loves her back.
I'd watch him from afar and fantasize
about the way his tongue would feel, his palms,
his summer breath, his hair between my fingers.

I'd give anything to have his love,

I whispered to the river and the moon.

II.

I got my wish. A giant catfish surfaced
one dusk along the Guadalupe's banks.

A galaxy of ripples swirled around
his body. *How about one night a month
you swim with me? He'll love you all the rest.
Let's seal our deal with a kiss,* he said.

One dirty night for twenty-nine of bliss?
Or an infinity of loneliness?

I felt his slimy whiskers on my cheek,
his smooth-as-river lips against my own.

I felt a slithering run up my leg;
I gasped in fear and knocked my knees together.

Now they'll stay that way all night,
                              he laughed.
And sure enough two legs became a fin.

By morning, you'll be normal once again,
and handsome Ollokot will long for you
with all of the desire you have for him.

But there's a catch. There always is in tales
like these. *No man can see your mermaid tail,*
one night a month you're mine and mine alone.

We traveled up and down the Guadalupe,
letting the current take us, hand in fin.

He led me to a dark secluded grotto
and there, we bathed in moonlight, river water,
love. Before the sun came up, my tail
morphed into legs again. I kissed my friend
goodbye, ran barefoot through the monte home.

III.

And sure enough, the man of my desires
was waiting in the village just for me.
That night, we kissed beneath a waning moon.
That night, we rolled in fields of firewheels.
That night, we drowned ourselves in paradise.

For twenty-eight more days, we lived in bliss.

What more could I want? My fantasy
became reality. My appetite
for love was satisfied. I savored him,
my Ollokot with tender hands, a voice
agave sweet, his eyes two hunter's moons
always on me. Delirious in love,
I forgot about my catfish friend
until the full moon showed her face again.

IV.

I hurried back into the Guadalupe,
dove in just before my legs could change
into a tail again. The murky water
hid my shameful secret as I swam
towards the bottom, looking for my catfish.

Ah, Sirena, princess of the river,
I've been dreaming of you all month long.

We swam together back to that same grotto,
where the moonlight shone through all the grime
and I could see his face beneath the surface.
His eyes fixated on my human half.

Sirena, do you dream of me on land?
Sirena, Ollokot can never love
you like I do, for all you are, from face
to tail. Sirena, stay with me forever.

His lips met mine. I pulled away, repulsed.
Of course I couldn't fall in love with him,
that monster from the depths. My heart belonged
to Ollokot. I swam away, my tail
flailing as I kicked up mud and waves.

V.

Come back, my love, he called into the night.
Don't swim that way, the mouth is dangerous!

I let the current carry me away,
hoping soon the sun would break the night
in two and I could leave this muddy river,
return to Ollokot's embrace. But then,

as the sky was blushing red, a hook
sliced through my tail. I wailed in pain and fear,
the river water turned from brown to mauve.
A net fell from the sky, ensnared my body.

I felt a tug and I was pulled ashore.
I flailed and flopped. My captor saw my body,
naked, glistening in the dawn. He shrieked.

I couldn't understand his words. His eyes
were like the ocean, wide and blue and deep.
He fixed them on my tail and shook his head
in disbelief. I hid my face in mud,
then felt his fingers on my tail, my skin.
I closed my eyes and willed the night's return.

VI.

When I awoke, a crowd of men surrounded
me, eyes wide and mouths agape. They gawked
and pointed at my tail, my naked breasts,
the lily pads entangled in my hair.
I glanced around the crowd, saw Ollokot.
My cheeks flushed red; he'd know my secret now.

Is it her? Another man asked him.
Ollokot looked at me in disgust.

This monster's not my wife. Just throw it back.

They lifted me with ease and tossed me in
the river like a fish that no one wants.
My body met the water with a splash,
and the current carried me away.
I watched my love grow smaller with the distance
as I drifted towards the river's mouth.

That's how I got here with this fish's tail.
I'll let the ocean swallow me, the gulf
promises to cover me in froth,
in waves, in solitude. Now that's my wish,
for no one else to gaze upon this body.
True love is just the stuff of fairy tales.
I'll write my happy ending in the sand.

Lobo Girl

The Legend of Lobo Girl

You want to hear a story? Well, ok,
just one, the candle's almost out, hermana.

About ten years ago, a couple lived
out by Devils River. Yeah, I know,
who would be so dumb to live out there?

Anyway, one stormy night the wife
went into labor and the husband left
to go get help. While on his way, a bolt
of lightning struck him dead. A pack of cowboys
found his body one day later, rode
out to his cabin to inform his wife.

They found her mangled corpse all chewed and clawed,
no baby anywhere. They figured lobos
devoured it, bones and all, and left no trace.

But little sis, the story doesn't end
just yet. We all forgot about the Dents
until a month ago. A woman saw
a pack of lobos munching on a goat,
but in their midst, she saw a naked girl,
on all fours, a beast with long black hair
and tufts of fur. Her face and teeth were stained
with rouge, with blood. She even growled and barked
when the senora got a little closer.

Yeah, that's right, the Lobo Girl's the baby.
She grew up wild with that pack of wolves,
and somehow morphed into an animal.

How's that possible, you ask? You know
a girl should never bathe in Devils River;
that's how diablos seeped into her skin
and turned her milkweed skin to furry hide.
As she slept beneath the leering moon,

the rays made her go loca. Now she walks
on palms and howls once the sun goes down.
You heard that too? The monte drove her mad.
A girl was never meant for wilderness,
so stay inside, ok? Oh, I forgot
my favorite part! She stalks Del Rio now,
looking for little girls who stay awake
past midnight. Why? Perhaps she'll steal them off
into the night and turn them feral like her,
perhaps she wants a taste of sweet young blood.
I can't be sure if now she's even human
anymore or if she's totally a monster.

But either way, hermana, say your prayers
and close your eyes. See, look, la vela's out.

Prairie Fire

Mrs. Palamara stood before
the entrance of our school each morning smoking
one last cigarette before the bell.

Like a sentinel, she'd guard the door,
inspecting every girl as she'd arrive,
scrutinizing every short skirt's hemline
for a flash of thigh, each plunging neckline
for a gleam of cleavage or the burst
of a bra strap, and ensuring every navel
was hidden underneath a shirt or blouse.

Her gaze burned fear in every girl. One morning,
I wore a brand new t-shirt, baby-blue,
the words in cursive, *Boys are stupid*, stretched
across my breasts. I felt the morning bell
breathing down my neck as I arrived,
the prairie of the schoolyard in full bloom
with blazing fuchsia clovers everywhere.

Mrs. P stood guard as usual
as ashes tumbled from her cigarette.
I felt the wind caress a slip of flesh
below my bellybutton as it blew
a cloud of dust between my face and hers.

Her eye became two slits on me. *You, girl,
Principal's office, now!* She screeched and snuffed
a flash of glowing ashes on the asphalt
with the heel of her leather boot.

That day, I went from just a teenage girl
to walking violation of the rules.
I had to wear a too-big scarlet polo,
faded, musty with the smell of smoke.

I wore it like a badge of shame and honor
my fire smoldering under Mrs. P's
control, for now, until she steps away.

The kindling was set, the tallgrass dry
and ready for a gust of summer's air.
A lightning spark of fingertips on skin
was all I needed for those flames to rage
out of control across that wind-swept schoolyard,
wild and burning out before my time.

Lobo Girl, the Cowboy's Love Story

He wanted this to be a fairy tale.
She needed rescue from the wilderness,
and he'd saved countless damsels without fail.
He pictured her, dolled up with tenderness,
her brambled hair untangled, all the burrs
combed out, her face scrubbed sparkling and pink.
She couldn't speak. It didn't matter, hers
was a language of yips and barks. He could think

enough for both of them, take care of her,
a gentle master, teach her how to be
lady-like, obedient, demure,
wait for him by the window sipping tea.
But in the dead of night, beneath the sheets,
she would be his animal, his beast.

Vigil for Persephone

What else is there left to do but lie
together, hand in hand, before the solstice?
My mother and I watch the ceiling fan
spin in endless motion as we savor
the fullness of our bellies and the taste
of Abuelita, cinnamon and pan
dulce lingering still on the tongue.

I've practiced my acceptance, packed away
sundresses, floppy gardening hats and chanclas.
I've let my hair grow long, the way he likes,
stopped polishing my nails a daisy color.
I've learned to love the fruits of winter, too—
calabaza in my empanadas,
grapefruit in the morning with some coffee,
tunas sliced thin, devoured seeds and all.

But my mother's different; she's a mom.
She puts the heater on full blast and shuts
her eyes. She tells herself it's always June,
that our time together is eternal
like her love. I know that once I'm gone,
she'll keep my bedroom as I've left it, rise
every morning, warm tortillas for two,
set the breakfast table and eat alone,
watch out the window for a trace of me.

Winter will take me with the coming sunrise.
My hand will slip from hers. I taste the bitter
sweetness of pomegranates on my tongue.

Lobo Girl Stalks the Vaquero

A vaquero shouldn't fear a wolf
but Lobo Girl's a wicked breed of beast.

Rumor is she howls at the moon.
She moves so fast that no one can escape
her foaming maw. A pack of wolves obey
her every bark, and she devours men
and cattle underneath the cloak of night—
a monster set on waste and desolation.

Her legend stalks him in his dreamsl; her growl
is every bitch's growl. Her blood-stained teeth
are every lady's pearly smile, her canines
penetrating muscle, bone and skin—
a ghost pain that his body never shakes.

Every rustle in the thicket fills
his throat with fear. Every gust of wind
carries his scent to her; she breathes him in.
She hides behind each firethorn bush, her eyes
two torches burning skin with lust and hunger.

She chills the young vaquero to the bone.
For once he feels like prey, a jackrabbit
ready to explode into a sprint.
A man should never feel this kind of terror.

Witness Report

We were only picking some flowers, honest,
by the fence where sunflowers grow the tallest.
We got lost. The coppice was like a labyrinth,
yellow with sunshine,

blooms and hair. We giggled and held hands, carefree,
rapt together, blissful and skipping through our
heaven. Then Persephone gazed beyond the
wall at a laurel

on the other side. It was full of blossoms.
*Wouldn't those look beautiful braided in your
hair?* she asked. *You'd be like a princess, lovely,
wearing a crown like*

that. Who wouldn't want to become a princess?
Percy leapt the fence in a single bound. She
flew so fast. I called out her name. She didn't
listen. I watched her

golden pigtails bounce with her movements as she
pulled the lowest limb to her level, plucked the
flowers by the fistful and stuffed them in her
pockets with fervor.

She was wild, delirious with this sudden
burst of freedom, wide-eyed and laughing, plucking.
As I watched, a part of me wished that I had
courage to join her,

but I feared the punishment we'd receive for
stepping off the bounds of the playground. *Scardy
cat,* she taunted me from the other side of
innocence. Then a

car pulled up, a chariot really, black and
shining, spewing clouds made of smoke. It honked and

roared. The driver called out her name. She turned,
looking back at me,

grinning as the passenger door swung open
like a portal leading to darkness. For a
moment, on the threshold, she stood there, staring
as I was pleading

for her not to leave me behind. She wasn't
scared. I saw her jump in the car and vanish
as the door slammed shut with a bang of thunder—
honest, I promise.

Eve's Diet Advice

I'm tired of commandments—thou shalt not
eat saturated fat. The carbohydrate
is the serpent in the grass. We're taught
that French fries are the enemy incarnate
to the gap between your thighs, a waist,
a butt that occupies no space. To be
an object of desire, you must embrace
eternal emptiness. Go gluten-free,

paleo or vegan. What baloney.
I eat what gives me pleasure, nothing more
or less. I eat what whets the tongue and only
what makes my toes curl back, what I adore,
what makes me dream of paradise, what feeds
the flesh that knows exactly what it needs.

How to Be a Woman in a Hostile World
Advice from Calamity Jane to her Daughter

This world will spit you out like spent tobacco
if you let it. Gals like us, the poor,
were made to spend our lives down on our knees,
barefoot, our tongues a useless piece of flesh.

But child, you have my blood within your veins,
which means you won't be satisfied with life
unless you spend it like a tumbleweed
in the wind, no roots to hold you down.
To find yourself you have to learn to break

the porcelain of your skin, the rules, your heart.
Cook breakfast for a lover as you smoke
a fat cigar. Wear rugged cowboy boots
beneath your petticoats so you can lift
your dress and run if danger strikes (it will).
Sing lullabies to orphans, air your lungs
out afterwards by cussing round the campfire.
Tend the sick and dying with your left
hand on the pearly pistol at your hip.

Lean on nothing but your own broad shoulders.
Be hero and be damsel of your tale,
the hopeful pioneer of your own heart.

The real calamity is wasting life
in the dust of someone else's wagon.
Trust your gut to lead you out of dodge,
and may your greatest sin be wanderlust.

My Husband Never Buys Me Flowers

I see them every Saturday, those men
cradling bouquets of fresh-cut flowers
in the grocery check-out line— dyed daisies,
carnations, or a single rose in rouge.

I'm emptying my shopping cart behind
one as he pays. He shifts inside his suit
taps a polished shoe, unsheathes his wallet,
disappears like mist into the night.

It's enough to make a gal feel cheated
out of romance. Isn't this what love
ought to look like: Men on tall white horses,
charming men with flowers in pressed suits,

men who slay the dragons, save the day?
I carry my own groceries to the car.
At home, my husband slumbers on the couch,
resting from another day of working

in the garden, trimming back the chaos
of the oak whose shade was suffocating
my marigolds. His open palms are blooming
with blisters like the petals of a rose.

Adam at Victoria's Secret

He wanders in the strange land like an exile
where everything is drenched in pink, each wall
the merchandise, his cheeks. And for a while,
he stands there, mouth agape, in awe at all

bras in every shade from milk to honey,
perfumes in every scent from tease to pear,
panties in every cut from thong to granny.
An angel, wearing just her underwear,

is plastered on the wall, a holy image
of femininity. She's curvy, thin;
she's pure and sexy all at once, what women
are taught to be. But Adam's wife is sin.

Her breasts are apple-sized. Her favorite color
is cherry red. She dresses just to please
herself. *What would you like to see your lover
in?* A saleswoman asks him, *These?*

She tempts him with a satin alabaster
cheekini in one hand, a lacy g-string
in the other. He frowns, this isn't her,
this cookie-cutter lingerie, she's nothing

like the mannequins, the models on
the walls. This paradise awash in pink
never really fit her sensuous brawn.
This isn't going to work. He'll have to think

of something else to please her on her birthday.
He thanks the saleswoman and once again
turns his back on Eden in dismay,
banished back into the world of men.

The Capture of Lobo Girl

Once upon a time, out by Del Rio,
a wild cowboy posse ganged together
to find the legendary Lobo Girl
and slay the big bad wolf within her heart.

Their quest went on for days. They searched the monte,
the towers of acacia trees, the dungeons
guarded by the groves of prickly pears.

They thrashed cenizo thickets into shreds
and trampled coppices of wildflowers
with their cowboy boots and horses' hooves.

A trail of foot and palm prints in caliche
lead them to the throat of Mile Canyon
then deep inside a cave. They heard a growl,
saw her lupine eyes, a flash of teeth.

She was their naked damsel in distress;
her body quaked with fear. She was alone.

The cowboys cornered her, one slipped his lasso
around her waist as easy as a ring
on a finger or a slipper on a foot.

He tugged her body close. She clawed his eye
and opened up her maw, let out a scream
that shook the canyon, echoed through the brush.

They heard a howl, the sound of paws on limestone.
A he-wolf bounded in and bared his teeth,
jumped the cowboy with the lasso, tore
into his arm. Another cowboy whipped
his pistol, shot the beast between the eyes.

Lobo Girl went faint. The cowboys tied
her extra tight, her brawny arms, her legs.

They'd never seen a woman quite so strong,
so wild, so full of fur. But nonetheless,
she was a lady needing rescue, princess
of the brush just waiting for her prince.
True love's kiss would surely make her change.

They carried her into her ever after.

Lobo Girl's Escape

She cowered in a corner of the room,
the darkest one, and watched them through the space
between her knees. They brought tortillas, water,
a quilt to cover up her nakedness.

A growl escaped her throat. What was this place?
Four walls, a tiny window, so much sound,
so many monsters lurking at the door,
knocking, peering, leering, shrieking, gasping.

No earth between her toes, no open sky,
no pack to snuggle up against at night.
She felt the space grow smaller by the second.
She felt her heart pound faster by the beat.

A moonbeam poured in through the window, touched
her cheek with tenderness, a tongue that wipes
away the putrid smell of this strange place.
At first she whimpered softly to herself,

longing to hide her face in someone's fur.
As she imagined home, her sobs grew louder.
Her fear exhaled with every heavy pant.
She opened up her jaws, let out a howl,

and then another, each one even louder
until the room resounded with her voice.
She stood up on her haunches, faced the moon
and felt the animal inside her chest

awaken once again. She roared and screamed, her voice
her only teeth against this enemy
called loneliness. And by some miracle,
another howl replied. Was it her echo

against the limestone hills? She answered back
a wail of hope. A louder howl replied

and filled her empty room and heart with life.
Soon there was a symphony of howls

crescendoing throughout Del Rio's streets.
The horses bucked. The goats began to bleat.
The women shrieked, and even all the cowboys
screamed in fear. A pack of lobos, hundreds,

stormed the city, growling, yipping, howling,
rushing towards the shack where she was held.
Amidst the chaos, she began to claw
the window with her paws and chew the wood.

She bashed her head, made fists, and threw her weight—
anything to escape. The window shattered,
wood split, and Lobo Girl breathed in the smell
of the wild, her home, and let the moonlight

warm her shivering flesh. She stood up straight,
surveyed the scene, the bedlam of the night
that she created with her voice, her pain.
She sealed her lips and bent down to the earth

on all fours once again. The monte called.
She disappeared into the shimmering distance.

Demeter, Just After the Winter Solstice

My story says that once my daughter leaves,
my heart was filled with grief and I was lost,

a wanderer, a hopeless mess of worry.
But let me tell you this: there's something sweet

about the sound of silence, how it wafts
through the hallways of this empty house,

how I can hear my own thoughts and my breath,
the sound of winter rustling the dying

leaves outside my bedroom window. Today,
I was awoken by my body's restful

satisfaction, not the blasting sound
of teenie-bopper music from her bedroom,

the constant rapping of her fingernails
on the keyboard, or her cellphone ringing

at the most ungodly hours. Today,
I didn't stumble on the thousand pairs

of shoes she always sloughs off from her feet
and leaves wherever they may fall like petals.

Today, there was no wad of umber hair
nestled in the shower drain, but still

those strands remain between the carpet threads,
on her pillowcase and in my mind.

Today, I'm walking naked through the house,
just a towel wrapped around my hair.

I'll drink a cup of coffee with no hurry.
What's the rush? There's nothing I can do

to bring her back, except to wait and let
the seasons have their way with both of us.

In March, she will return a different woman.
We'll share a bottle of merlot and laugh

about the fleeting seasons, how to find
our pleasures as they thunder past us all.

My Suegra's Molcajete

My suegra sets her molcajete out
on the counter, tells me that it's time
I learned to use it like a real woman.

Mira, mija, learn a thing or two.

She throws a toasted chile in the bowl
along with two tomatoes, their red skin
blistered, wrinkled, like a sun-burnt brow.

A tejolote in one hand, my suegra
cradles the molcajete as she grinds.

She has an urgency about her movement,
the way she teaches me as if today
is the day I have to learn it all
how to take her place, to fill this kitchen
with her commanding presence and her grace.

I have a lot to learn, I'm far from perfect.
My hands still hesitate at the comal,
I flip tortillas with a spatula,
and I'm afraid to skin the prickly pears
she plucks from our backyard with bravery.

My palms are smooth, the seeds of jalepenos
make them burn and redden like the sun.

My suegra passes me the tejolote
She heaves a sigh of pure exhaustion, sits
down at the bar. Her tired body sinks.

You try, mijita. I'll sit here and watch.

I grind the stone against the stone, a little
slow at first. My suegra nods, approves,

Rapidamente, use your muscles, child.

My wrist begins to dance, the flavors mix,
the hues of the tomato and serrano
blend into a muted sunset red.

A liberal shake of salt, a squirt of lime,
I finish as my hand begins to ache.

I spoon a little on a warm tortilla
de maiz and nod my head. *Not hot,*
I say and suck in air across my tongue.

This is a salsa that she'll never try.

How does it taste? she asks, imagining
the heat, remembering the countless batches
she used to slather over everything
before the chemo therapy that ravaged
her stomach and her appetite for life.

*Delicious, with a bit of garlic flavor,
where's that from?*

          *The molcajete carries
with it everything, the flavors of
the past,* she says and grins, *and now I pass
it all to you. It's yours.* It seems I'm worthy
of this basalt bowl that time has seasoned
with ajo, sal, limon, the molcajete
her grandma gave her just before she died,
the heavy, awkward thing my suegra carried
in her arms from Torreon to Texas.
It didn't fit inside her single suitcase,
but she couldn't bear the thought of leaving
it behind. I know I'm not the daughter
she imagined with my clumsy tongue
a nervous pair of hands, a will to work
outside the home, a gringa from up north
who uses blenders, orders take-out, writes,

but still I'll carry on this molcajete,
a tradition I'll give to my daughter
whose values will be different from my own.
I'll explain the journey of our past,
the nuance of the culture that we are,
how it comes together, blends to make
a perfect salsa, mixed together in
the Great Americano Molcajete.

Spring Cleaning After Eden

In a perfect world, homes clean themselves.
There are no epic battles waged between
dust and vacuum cleaners, mud and mops,
order and chaos. *Who could live in such
a place,* she wonders as she thinks of Eden,
how her hands were idle, how she tiptoed
through a home she never felt she owned.
Here, the clutter's hers and hers alone

to clear. She is the savior of this home,
the one who sweeps the cat hair, scrubs the stains
that mar her countertops, fills up the trash,
with yesterday's mistakes: the empty bag
of potato chips, the crumpled letters
of apology the size of fists,
the bitten apple core that's turning umber.
She fills the trash and Adam rises up
from his Easy Chair, lets out a grunt
and takes it to the curb. His work is done.

Eve puts her hands on hips and heaves a sigh,
declares this tidy paradise their own.

Paean to the Pear on the Kitchen Counter

Shaved and sweetened coconuts. Slender apple
slices, tart and slipping between two trembling
lips. A mango, glistening on a stick. A
cup overflowing—

watermelon, cantaloupe, honey dew, all
seeded, diced, a dust of chamoy, a squirt of
lime to whet the appetite, make the mouth flood
full of saliva

Hauled and chopped up strawberries drenched in cream with
sugar sprinkled everywhere, sparkling like
lip gloss, dressed up, ready to fill the hunger,
made for your pleasure

All of this to simply enjoy some fruit! But
what about the pear on the kitchen counter,
ripe and dressed in nothing but skin? There is no
joy like the sudden

touch to lips, spontaneous bite, surprise of
dulcet juice that's dribbling down the chin, the
neck, the chest, the splitting of skin. You swallow
seeds and devour

sweetness by the mouthful. You eat the core, the
stem, the blemishes and the earth. You keep it
simple, pure, and impulsive. Let's make love with
that kind of passion

Lobo Girl's Advice to Ladies

I sniff your dainty footprints in the dust,
listen for your voice amidst the bustle,
and see you gazing at the eyelash moon,
swallowing the howl in your throat.
I hear your husband whistle; you obey.
I watch him raise his hand and see you cower.

Are you happy locked inside that cage
you call a dress? I wonder if you dream
of breaking free, of sloughing off your skirt,
of tearing through the bodices of rules
that keep you small and terrified like prey.

Come a little closer to the darkness.
Let me take your hand within my paw.
I'll teach you that you're tougher than you think.
Skin can callous; muscles bloom with use
like dogwood flowers after thunderstorms.
The canines in your mouth are just like mine.
You have to learn to bare them with a snarl.

I'm not the big bad wolf you're taught to fear.
Come with me and let me introduce
you to the beast behind your fiery eyes.

La Luna

The Woman in the Moon

I used to gaze up at the moon with pity—
a woman there alone for centuries
casting rays of moonlight on the city
as lovers stroll and kiss, make memories
she'll never have. What worse fate could there be?
Such coldness, silence, so much dust, a face
furrowed by years of loneliness at sea,
orbiting through the empty depths of space.

Today, as darkness falls, I understand.
She is the brightest body in this dead
of night. She takes up space; she's full and grand.
Shamelessly, she shimmers, bold in red.
She smirks with lips of regolith, her eye
a crater, winking at me from the sky.

Critics on *The Garden, Uprooted*

"With her deft, sensuous, jaunty, and vital poems Katie Hoerth makes a smart debut. The poet mixes fairy tale images with visceral descriptions in this sexy—and crafted—first book that keeps turning preconceptions inside out."

Molly Peacock, author of *The Paper Garden* and *The Second Blush*

"Ripeness is all" in these poems where mangoes, melons, and pomegranates redden and fall into the dry soil of south Texas to be eaten, to rot, or to bury their seeds. *The Garden, Uprooted* is a debut collection from a young poet to watch."

Julie Kane, Lousiana Poet Laureate and author of *Jazz Funeral* and *Rhythm and Booze*

"*The Garden, Uprooted* is a fall into love, with all the trepidation and exhilaration of your first parachute jump. These poems are a sumptuous feast. They will fulfill your longing for pleasure. "

Steven Schneider, author of *The Magic of the Mariachi*, *Unexpected Guests*, and *Borderlines: Drawing Border Lives*

"*The Garden, Uprooted* is a hypnotic burlesque dance, a garden frenzy of delights...And yet, the truth is here too, revealed in bursting metamorphoses and greatly impacted by the gradually seen and unseen realities of South Texas. It is because the poet is a Northern tree in foreign soil that the Texas-Mexico border so evocatively demands that she, like other border-dwellers, eternally ask, 'Who am I?' and 'Where do I belong?'"

ire'ne lara silva, author of *furia* and *blood sugar canto*

Critics on *Goddess Wears Cowboy Boots*

"The strength of this collection lies in pitch-perfect metaphors scaffolded on the most everyday objects... Grocery stores, deserts, and high school football fields provide a perfect backdrop for cosmological dramas – and the rugged men and women Hoerth portrays are indeed a match for gods."

Coal Hill Review

"Every poem in Katherine Hoerth's *Goddess Wears Cowboy Boots* is a fresh gust of wind. In this stunning collection, Hoerth deconstructs the complexity of femininity, and the steep binary that makes feminine beauty both dangerous and powerful, sinful and godly. These poems are effortlessly steeped in nature and mythology, and each is as satisfying as Eve's first taste of forbidden fruit."

Pank

"Katherine Hoerth ... is clearly a rising star. Ripe with carefully constructed rhythms amidst the free verse, memorable imagery and deft, assured wordplay, *Goddess Wears Cowboy Boots* is the work of a poet who's fully come in to her own."

David Bowles for *The Monitor*

"Katherine Hoerth writes poems that lovers of poetry will admire, fans of stories will enjoy, and poets will find astonishing for the poetic mastery in the integration of form and meaning."

Jerry Craven, author of *Ceremonial Stones of Fire*, *Women of Thunder*, and *Becoming Others*

www.ingramcontent.com/pod-product-compliance
Lightning Source LLC
LaVergne TN
LVHW091228080426
835509LV00009B/1210